Thank you...

... for purchasing this copy of Get Ready for Year 4.

We hope that you will find the book helpful in preparing your child to move up to their next year-group. You may choose to use it during the final few months of Year 3, during summer holidays or in the first few months of Year 4.

On our Teachers and Parents pages we summarise the likely content of each subject in Year 4. On the children's pages we feature activities that will help prepare children for most of their subjects, hopefully giving them confidence to take part in their lessons with enthusiasm, skills and knowledge.

This book is part of our growing range of educational titles. Most of our books are individual workbooks but, due to popular demand, we are now introducing a greater number of photocopiable titles especially for teachers.

To find details of our other publications, please visit our website:

www.acblack.com

CONTENTS

Get Ready for Year 4

During the course of Year 4, your children will learn mathematics every day in the Numeracy Hour. They will be taught to:

- ✔ Learn to use the symbols < (less than) and > (greater than).

- ✔ Round numbers, up to 1000, to the nearest 10 or 100.

- ✔ Work with fractions such as $\frac{3}{4}$, $\frac{2}{3}$, $\frac{5}{8}$ and with 'mixed numbers' such as $2\frac{1}{2}$ and $1\frac{3}{4}$.

- ✔ Add and subtract numbers mentally. (For example, adding 37 and 24, subtracting 24 from 37. Addition and subtraction facts to 20. Use additions to make 100, e.g. 72+28, 50+50, 70+30, etc.)

- ✔ Add together numbers less than 1000 by arranging them in appropriate columns (including more than two numbers).

- ✔ Arrange numbers less than 1000 in columns to carry out subtraction.

- ✔ Know the 2,3,4,5 and 10 times tables, and begin learning 6,7,8,9.

- ✔ Work out division facts from the 2,3,4,5 and 10 times tables.

- ✔ Work out remainders from divisions.

- ✔ Use units of length: millimetres(mm), centimetres(cm), metres(m), kilometres(km).

- ✔ Use units of mass: grams(g), kilograms(kg).

- ✔ Use units of capacity: millilitres(ml), litres(l).

- ✔ Recognise features of two dimensional shapes including whether they are regular, whether they are symmetrical, whether they have right angles.

- ✔ Solve problems using numbers.

- ✔ Use eight compass directions N, S, W, E, SE, NW, SW and NE.

On the next twelve pages we provide activities to strengthen children's abilities in handling numbers and to introduce some of the prerequisites for learning the aspects of maths listed above. The children may need help with some of the questions.

GREATER THAN AND LESS THAN.

I have two fish...

... but I have more!

We can write : 2 < 4

The crocodile always faces the biggest number.

this means 'is less than' so we say: two is less than four

OR

4 > 2

this means 'is more than' so we say: four is greater than two

Write < or > in the boxes to make these statements true. You already know how to do the first two questions.

#		#		#		#		#		#	
1. 4		2	3. 8		6	5. 23		30			
2. 2		4	4. 6		8	6. 30		23			

#		#		#		#		#		#	
7. 17		21	9. 15		14	11. 0		1			
8. 21		17	10. 14		15	12. 1		0			

#		#		#		#		#		#	
13. 70		7	15. 99		88	17. 118		119			
14. 7		70	16. 88		99	18. 119		118			

#		#		#		#		#		#	
19. 165		516	21. 300		150	23. 820		208			
20. 516		165	22. 150		300	24. 208		820			

#		#		#		#		#		#	
25. 123		312	28. 247		472	31. 856		865			
26. 213		132	29. 724		742	32. 685		658			
27. 321		231	30. 427		274	33. 568		586			

ROUNDING TO THE NEAREST TEN.

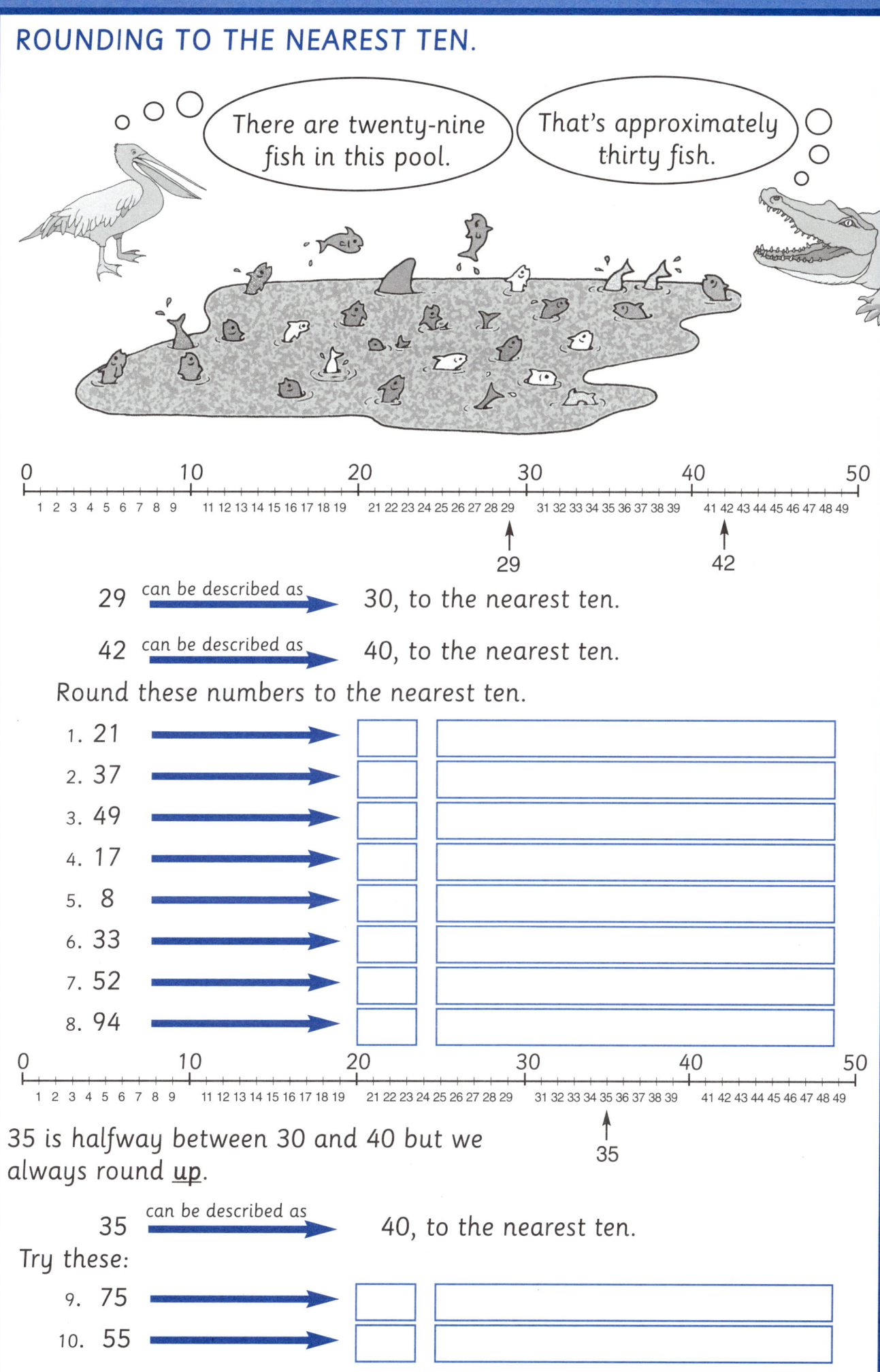

There are twenty-nine fish in this pool.

That's approximately thirty fish.

0   10   20   30   40   50

1 2 3 4 5 6 7 8 9   11 12 13 14 15 16 17 18 19   21 22 23 24 25 26 27 28 29   31 32 33 34 35 36 37 38 39   41 42 43 44 45 46 47 48 49

↑ 29   ↑ 42

29 can be described as → 30, to the nearest ten.

42 can be described as → 40, to the nearest ten.

Round these numbers to the nearest ten.

1. 21 →
2. 37 →
3. 49 →
4. 17 →
5. 8 →
6. 33 →
7. 52 →
8. 94 →

0   10   20   30   40   50

1 2 3 4 5 6 7 8 9   11 12 13 14 15 16 17 18 19   21 22 23 24 25 26 27 28 29   31 32 33 34 35 36 37 38 39   41 42 43 44 45 46 47 48 49

↑ 35

35 is halfway between 30 and 40 but we always round **up**.

35 can be described as → 40, to the nearest ten.

Try these:

9. 75 →
10. 55 →

FRACTIONS

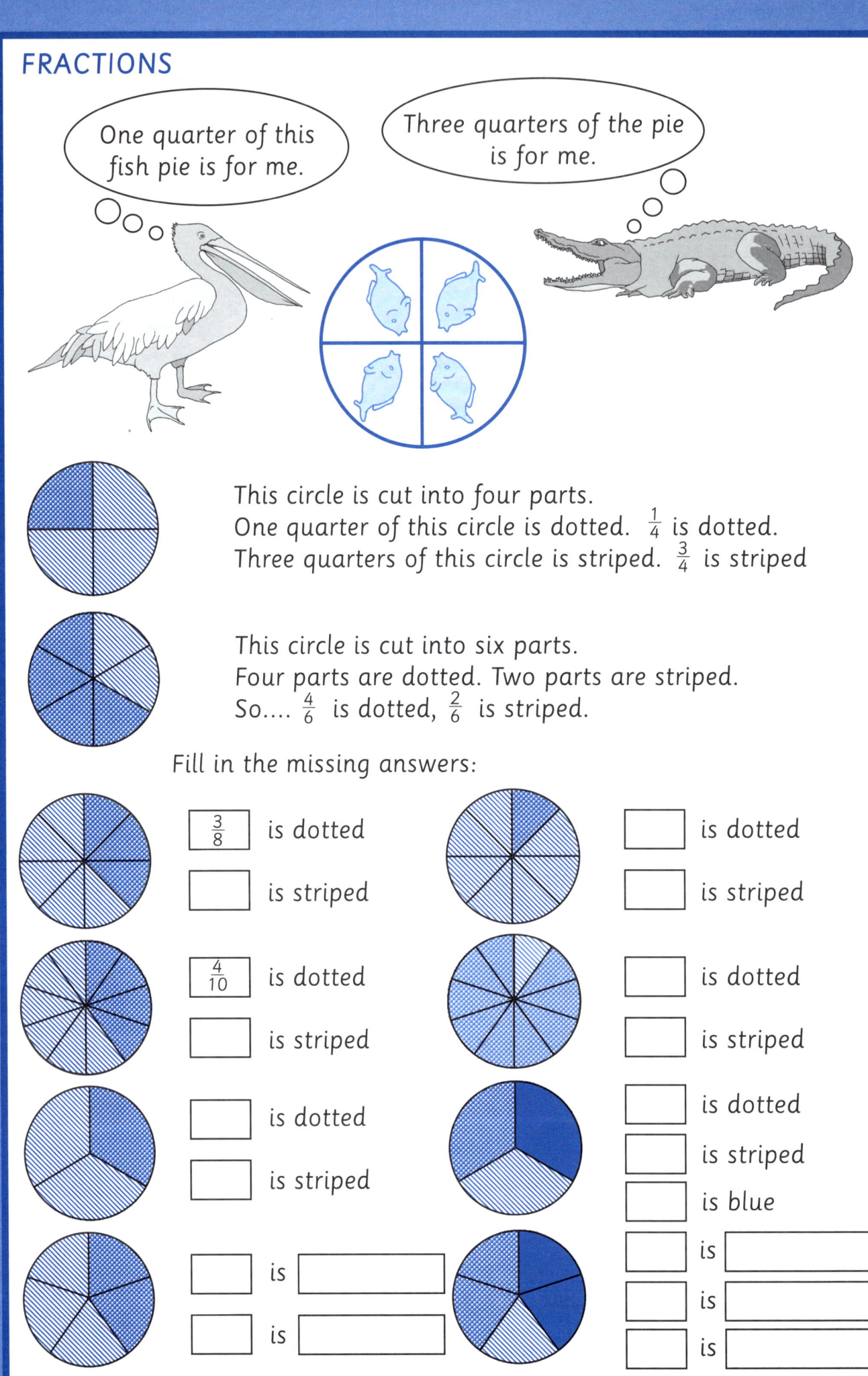

One quarter of this fish pie is for me.

Three quarters of the pie is for me.

This circle is cut into four parts.
One quarter of this circle is dotted. $\frac{1}{4}$ is dotted.
Three quarters of this circle is striped. $\frac{3}{4}$ is striped

This circle is cut into six parts.
Four parts are dotted. Two parts are striped.
So.... $\frac{4}{6}$ is dotted, $\frac{2}{6}$ is striped.

Fill in the missing answers:

$\frac{3}{8}$ is dotted

☐ is striped

☐ is dotted

☐ is striped

$\frac{4}{10}$ is dotted

☐ is striped

☐ is dotted

☐ is striped

☐ is dotted

☐ is striped

☐ is dotted

☐ is striped

☐ is blue

☐ is ☐

☐ is ☐

☐ is ☐

☐ is ☐

Get Ready for Year 4 Numeracy

Fractions

MAKING 100.

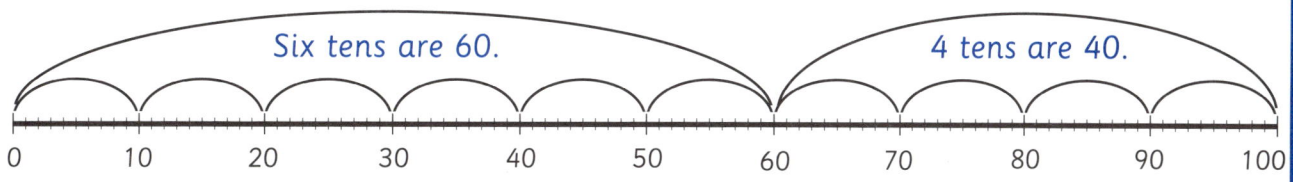

$$60 \qquad + \qquad 40 \qquad = \qquad 100$$

Six tens are 60.

4 tens are 40.

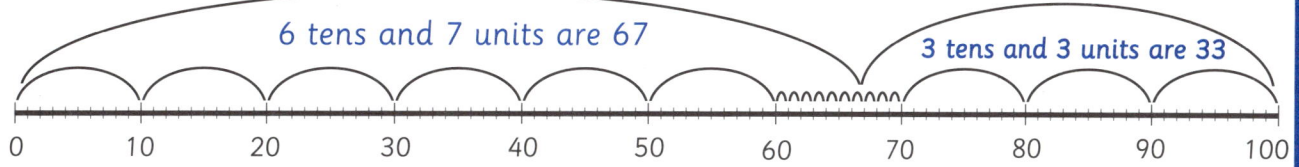

$$67 \qquad + \qquad 33 \qquad = \qquad 100$$

6 tens and 7 units are 67

3 tens and 3 units are 33

You can use this number line to help you with the questions below.

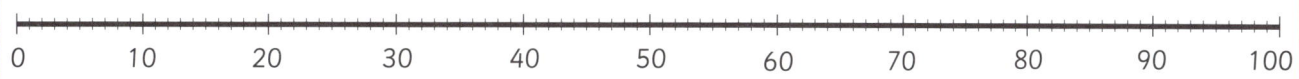

1. 70 + ☐ = 100	2. 20 + ☐ = 100	3. 90 + ☐ = 100
4. 40 + ☐ = 100	5. 50 + ☐ = 100	6. 80 + ☐ = 100
7. 30 + ☐ = 100	8. 10 + ☐ = 100	9. 60 + ☐ = 100

10. 51 + ☐ = 100   Be careful. The answer is <u>not</u> 59.

11. 75 + ☐ = 100   Be careful. The answer is <u>not</u> 35.

12. 67 + ☐ = 100	13. 22 + ☐ = 100	14. 1 + ☐ = 100
15. 44 + ☐ = 100	16. 82 + ☐ = 100	17. 77 + ☐ = 100
18. 13 + ☐ = 100	19. 36 + ☐ = 100	20. 98 + ☐ = 100

LENGTH

This line is one millimetre long.

This line is one centimetre long.

You can see that ten millimetres equal one centimetre.

We write **10mm = 1 cm**.

Fill in the missing numbers:

1. 20mm = ☐ cm   2. 40mm = ☐ cm   3. 70mm = ☐ cm

4. 8cm = ☐ mm   5. 6cm = ☐ mm   6. 12cm = ☐ mm

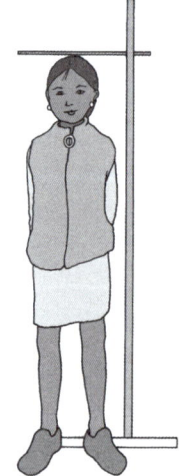

Jasdeep is exactly one metre tall.

One metre = one hundred centimetres

1m = 100cm

Fill in the missing numbers:

1. 2m = ☐ cm   2. 4m = ☐ cm   3. 500cm = ☐ m

4. 300cm = ☐ m   5. 1/2m = ☐ cm   6. 1/4m = ☐ cm

ADDITION

If you want to add numbers together...

..it's sometimes easier to write them in columns.

Hundreds   Tens   Units

$$\begin{array}{r} 3\ 4\ 7 \\ +\ 1\ 3\ 6 \\ \hline \end{array}$$

Look: 347 + 136 →

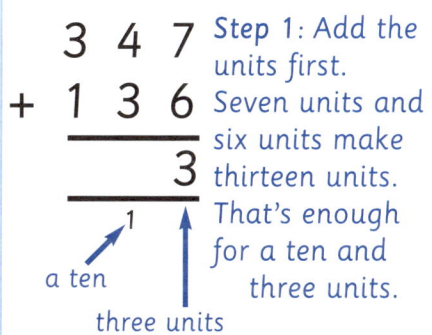

Step 1: Add the units first. Seven units and six units make thirteen units. That's enough for a ten and three units.

a ten

three units

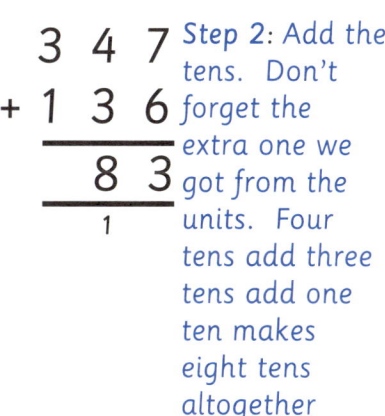

Step 2: Add the tens. Don't forget the extra one we got from the units. Four tens add three tens add one ten makes eight tens altogether

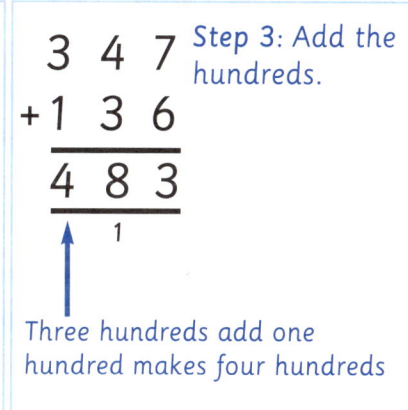

Step 3: Add the hundreds.

Three hundreds add one hundred makes four hundreds

Now try these additions by writing the numbers in columns.

1. 218 + 135

2. 421 + 234

3. 329 + 37

Look. We have put the biggest number first.

4. 219 + 28 + 346

$$\begin{array}{r} 3\ 4\ 6 \\ 2\ 1\ 9 \\ +\ 2\ 8 \\ \hline \end{array}$$

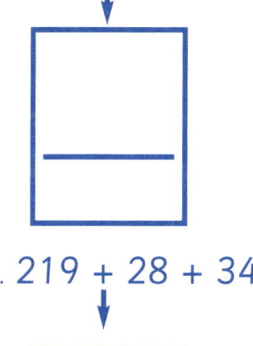

5. 307 + 448 + 9

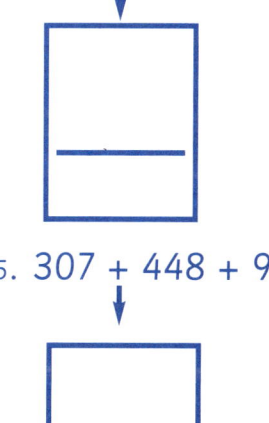

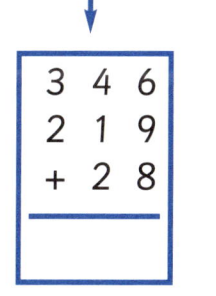

SUBTRACTION

Last year there were four hundred and sixty-eight fish in the pond...

...and I ate two hundred and thirty-three of them!

How many fish are left?
There were 468.   Crocodile ate 233.

Step 1. Subtract the units.	Step 2. Subtract the tens.	Step 3. Subtract the hundreds.
$\begin{array}{r} 4\ 6\ 8 \\ -\ 2\ 3\ 3 \\ \hline 5 \end{array}$ Eight units subtract three units gives five units.	$\begin{array}{r} 4\ 6\ 8 \\ -\ 2\ 3\ 3 \\ \hline 3\ 5 \end{array}$ Six tens subtract three tens gives three tens.	$\begin{array}{r} 4\ 6\ 8 \\ -\ 2\ 3\ 3 \\ \hline 2\ 3\ 5 \end{array}$ Four hundreds subtract two hundreds gives two hundreds.

Now try these subtractions by writing the numbers in columns:

1. 675 − 214

2. 893 − 512

3. 487 − 53

4. 999 − 625

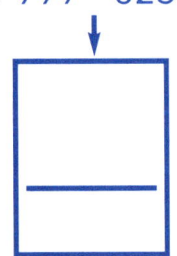

5. 767 − 215

6. 844 − 332

QUICK QUESTIONS

How fast can you do these additions and subtractions?

How fast can I eat a pelican?

1 Quick Additions

3 + 7 =

8 + 4 =

9 + 6 =

8 + 7 =

5 + 9 =

Time taken ☐ seconds

4 Quick Subtractions

20 – 6 =

20 – 2 =

20 – 8 =

20 – 7 =

20 – 3 =

Time taken ☐ seconds

7 Quick Mix

14 + 6 =

20 – 6 =

5 + 9 =

16 – 7 =

6 + 4 =

10 – 4 =

12 + 8 =

20 – 12 =

20 – 8 =

8 + 2 =

7 + 6 =

13 – 6 =

9 + 5 =

14 – 9 =

8 + 9 =

17 – 8 =

17 – 9 =

10 + 9 =

19 – 10 =

16 – 8 =

Time taken ☐ seconds

2

6 + 6 =

9 + 9 =

8 + 8 =

7 + 7 =

5 + 5 =

Time taken ☐ seconds

5

15 – 6 =

15 – 9 =

15 – 8 =

15 – 7 =

15 – 11 =

Time taken ☐ seconds

3

15 + 4 =

12 + 6 =

14 + 3 =

11 + 5 =

13 + 7 =

Time taken ☐ seconds

6

12 – 7 =

12 – 6 =

12 – 8 =

12 – 5 =

12 – 4 =

Time taken ☐ seconds

MULTIPLICATION TABLES

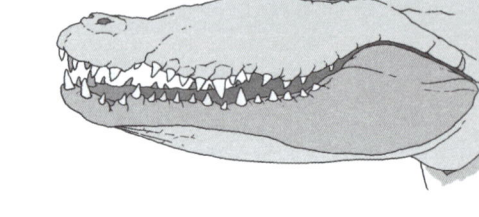

Do you know your tables?

I know what a coffee table is.

Complete these multiplication tables as fast as you can.
Check your answers by looking inside the back cover of the book.

| 1 x 2 = |
| 2 x 2 = |
| 3 x 2 = |
| 4 x 2 = |
| 5 x 2 = |
| 6 x 2 = |
| 7 x 2 = |
| 8 x 2 = |
| 9 x 2 = |
| 10 x 2 = |

| 1 x 3 = |
| 2 x 3 = |
| 3 x 3 = |
| 4 x 3 = |
| 5 x 3 = |
| 6 x 3 = |
| 7 x 3 = |
| 8 x 3 = |
| 9 x 3 = |
| 10 x 3 = |

| 1 x 4 = |
| 2 x 4 = |
| 3 x 4 = |
| 4 x 4 = |
| 5 x 4 = |
| 6 x 4 = |
| 7 x 4 = |
| 8 x 4 = |
| 9 x 4 = |
| 10 x 4 = |

| 1 x 5 = |
| 2 x 5 = |
| 3 x 5 = |
| 4 x 5 = |
| 5 x 5 = |
| 6 x 5 = |
| 7 x 5 = |
| 8 x 5 = |
| 9 x 5 = |
| 10 x 5 = |

| 1 x 10 = |
| 2 x 10 = |
| 3 x 10 = |
| 4 x 10 = |
| 5 x 10 = |
| 6 x 10 = |
| 7 x 10 = |
| 8 x 10 = |
| 9 x 10 = |
| 10 x 10 = |

MORE MULTIPLICATION TABLES

1	x	6	=	6	add 6
2	x	6	=	12	add 6
3	x	6	=	18	
4	x	6	=	☐	
5	x	6	=	☐	
6	x	6	=	☐	
7	x	6	=	☐	
8	x	6	=	☐	
9	x	6	=	☐	
10	x	6	=	☐	

1	x	7	=	7
2	x	7	=	☐
3	x	7	=	☐
4	x	7	=	☐
5	x	7	=	☐
6	x	7	=	☐
7	x	7	=	☐
8	x	7	=	☐
9	x	7	=	☐
10	x	7	=	☐

1	x	8	=	8
2	x	8	=	☐
3	x	8	=	☐
4	x	8	=	☐
5	x	8	=	☐
6	x	8	=	☐
7	x	8	=	☐
8	x	8	=	☐
9	x	8	=	☐
10	x	8	=	☐

1	x	9	=	9
2	x	9	=	☐
3	x	9	=	☐
4	x	9	=	☐
5	x	9	=	☐
6	x	9	=	☐
7	x	9	=	☐
8	x	9	=	☐
9	x	9	=	☐
10	x	9	=	☐

DIVIDING NUMBERS

If I share twelve fish between three pelicans...

... they will get four fish each.

Look: 12 ÷ 3 = 4

because 3 x 4 = 12   or   4 x 3 = 12

You can use your multiplication tables to find the answers to division questions.

Try these:

1 18 ÷ 2 =   2 36 ÷ 4 =   3 24 ÷ 6 =

4 30 ÷ 5 =   5 28 ÷ 7 =   6 50 ÷ 10 =

7 16 ÷ 2 =   8 18 ÷ 3 =   9 27 ÷ 3 =

10 45 ÷ 5 =   11 32 ÷ 8 =   12 45 ÷ 9 =

13 If there are 20 fish, how many can 4 pelicans have each?

14 If I have £72 to share equally between 9 people, how much can they have each?

15 I have 32 sweets to share equally between 4 children. How many can they have each?

USING MEASURING CYLINDERS

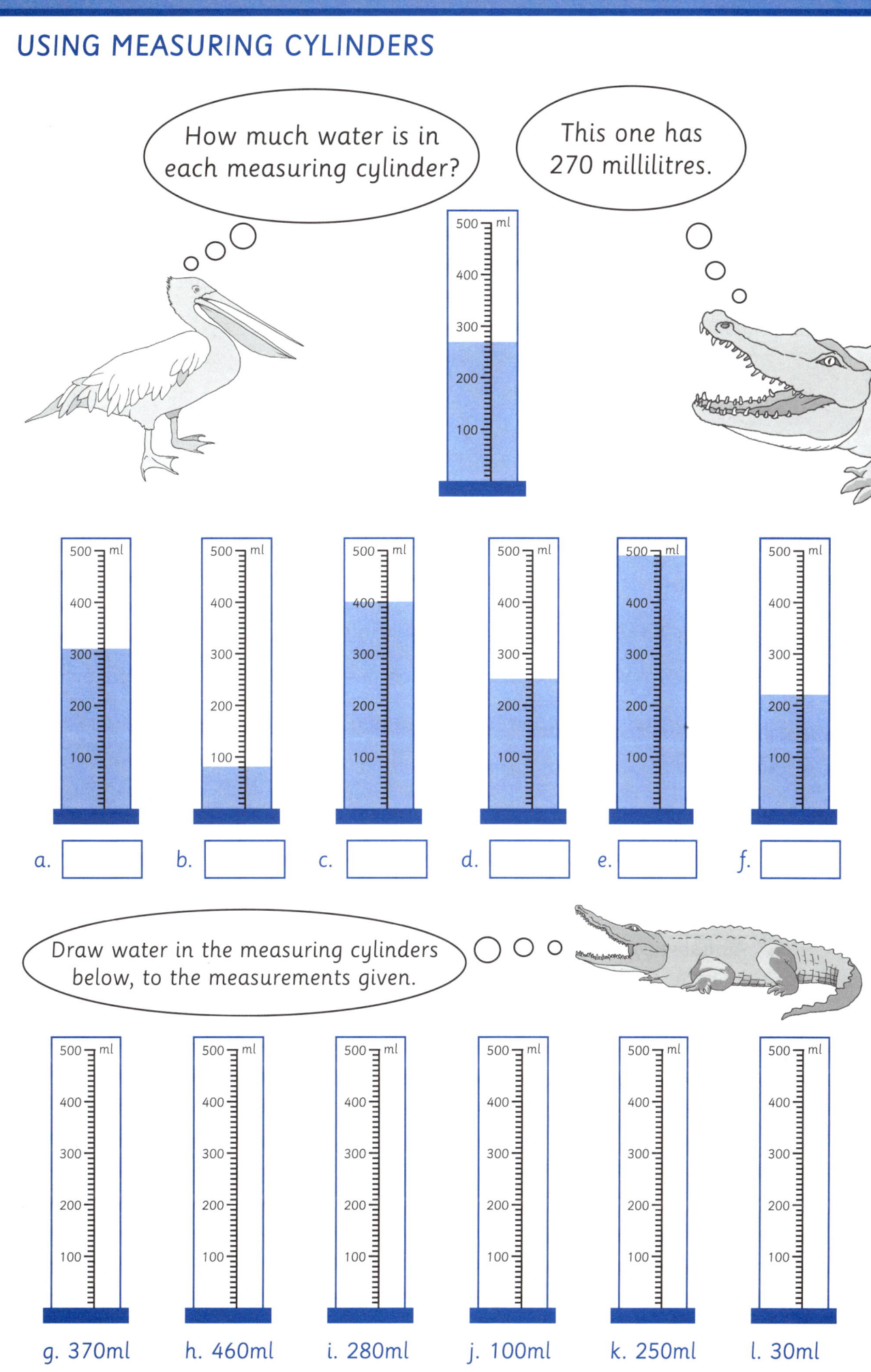

How much water is in each measuring cylinder?

This one has 270 millilitres.

a. [ ]   b. [ ]   c. [ ]   d. [ ]   e. [ ]   f. [ ]

Draw water in the measuring cylinders below, to the measurements given.

g. 370ml   h. 460ml   i. 280ml   j. 100ml   k. 250ml   l. 30ml

During their literacy work in Year 4, your children will build on the work they have done in Years 1 to 3. They will experience the daily Literacy Hour, in which they may read texts guided by their teachers and learn about aspects of grammar, spelling and writing. The lessons will include work on:

- ✔ Verb tenses.

- ✔ Using powerful verbs.

- ✔ Adverbs.

- ✔ Comparative adjectives.

- ✔ Commas.

- ✔ Spelling strategies, including recognising a range of common letter strings, double consonants, common prefixes and suffixes and following a **learn, write, check** approach to learning spellings.

- ✔ Using clear, correctly formed, joined handwriting.

- ✔ Possessive apostrophes.

- ✔ Making short notes from a full text.

- ✔ The importance of word order in a sentence.

- ✔ Alphabetical order, sorted by the third letter and beyond.

- ✔ Use of dictionary and thesaurus.

- ✔ Understanding the terms rhyming couplet, verse, chorus and alliteration.

- ✔ Counting the syllables in lines of poetry.

- ✔ Writing character sketches.

- ✔ Reading and performing play scripts.

Introductory work for many of the above points will be found in the literacy pages in this book.

TECHNICAL VOCABULARY

You should understand the meanings of all the words in the box below.

noun	tense	syllable	verb
adverb	alliteration		prefix
rhyme	suffix		adjective

Now choose the correct word from the box to solve each of the clues below. If you get stuck, use a dictionary to help you.

1. A word <u>ending</u> such as **ly**, **ant** or **ment**. _ _ _ _ _ _

2. A 'doing' word. _ _ _ _

3. Words with a similar sound at the end, e.g. **night, fright**. _ _ _ _ _

4. A sound or beat within a word. _ _ _ _ _ _ _ _

5. A word which describes a verb. _ _ _ _ _ _

6. A word which describes a noun. _ _ _ _ _ _ _ _ _

7. Words which sound the same at the beginning, e.g. **she shall shine shoes**. _ _ _ _ _ _ _ _ _ _ _ _

8. Past, present or future _ _ _ _ _

9. A naming word. _ _ _ _

10. A word beginning, such as **al**, **in** or **ad** _ _ _ _ _ _

SYLLABLES

Words can be split into syllables.
Write the number of syllables in each of the words below. Try reading them out loud, you may find it easier to hear the syllables. The first few are done for you.

night (1)	sun (1)	shining (2)	carpenter (3)
billows ( )	middle ( )	sulkily ( )	spoil ( )
walrus ( )	overhead ( )	incredible ( )	seven ( )
conveniently ( )	quantities ( )	and ( )	eager ( )

Read this poem by the famous author Lewis Carroll who lived from 1832 to 1898.
Write the number of syllables at the end of each line. The first one has been done for you.

The Walrus and the Carpenter

The sun was shining on the sea,   (8)
Shining with all his might: ( )
He did his very best to make   ( )
The billows smooth and bright –   ( )
And this was odd because it was   ( )
The middle of the night   ( )

The moon was shining sulkily,   ( )
Because she thought the sun   ( )
Had got no business to be there   ( )
After the day was done –   ( )
"It's very rude of him," she said,   ( )
"To come and spoil the fun!"   ( )

Did you notice the pattern in the number of syllables in each line?

RHYMING COUPLETS

When two successive lines of a verse end with rhyming words it is called a rhyming couplet.

Choose words from the box to complete each of these rhyming couplets. You will not need all the words.

here	tea	ladder	tree
wall	dreaming	sky	door
standing	day	there	banana

I like to sit beside the sea,
And there I eat my picnic _ _ _

In summer the scent of the newly mown hay
Floats through the air on a warm sunny _ _ _

One, two, three, four,
Someone knocked upon the _ _ _ _

A, B, C, D,
Climb a tall _ _ _ _

Mirror on the wall so clear,
Tell me who is standing _ _ _ _

She thought the fright would start her screaming,
But she woke up, as she had just been _ _ _ _ _ _ _ _

APOSTROPHES

An apostrophe can be used to make two words into one.

e.g.   could not ⟶ couldn't
       would not ⟶ wouldn't

An apostrophe can also be used to show belonging.

e.g.   The toy belonging to the dog ⟶ The dog's toy.
       The banana belonging to the girl ⟶ The girl's banana.

Write these phrases and sentences again, using apostrophes.

1.   The book belonging to the boy.

     _____

2.   She was not very good at knitting.

     _____

3.   The pencil-case owned by my friend.

     _____

4.   The engine belonging to the car.

     _____

5.   The trousers that are owned by my dad.

     _____

6.   I will not go out today.

     _____

7.   The earrings belonging to my sister.

     _____

8.   He could not tie his shoelace.

     _____

Page 4   GREATER THAN AND LESS THAN

1.>, 2.<, 3.>, 4.<, 5.<, 6.>, 7.<, 8.>, 9.>, 10.<, 11.<, 12.>,13.>, 14.<, 15.>, 16.<, 17.<, 18.>, 19.<, 20.>, 21.>, 22.<, 23.>, 24.<, 25.<, 26.>, 27.>, 28.<, 29.<, 30.>,31.<, 32.>, 33.<.

Page 5   ROUNDING TO THE NEAREST TEN

20 to the nearest ten.40, 50, 20, 10, 30, 50, 90. 80 to the nearest ten, 60 to the nearest ten.

Page 6   FRACTIONS

$\frac{5}{8}$ is striped, $\frac{1}{8}$ is dotted, $\frac{7}{8}$ is striped.
$\frac{6}{10}$ is striped, $\frac{9}{10}$ is dotted, $\frac{1}{10}$ is striped.
$\frac{1}{3}$ is dotted, $\frac{2}{3}$ is striped.
$\frac{1}{3}$ is dotted, $\frac{1}{3}$ is striped, $\frac{1}{3}$ is blue.
$\frac{2}{5}$ is dotted, $\frac{3}{5}$ is striped.
$\frac{2}{5}$ is blue, $\frac{2}{5}$ is dotted, $\frac{1}{5}$ is striped.

Page 7   MAKING 100

30,80,10,60,50,20,70,90,40,49,25,33,78,99,56 18,23,87,64,2.

Page 8   LENGTH

2cm, 4cm, 7cm, 80mm, 60mm, 120mm 200cm, 400cm, 5m, 3m, 50cm, 25cm.

Page 9   ADDITION

353, 655, 366, 593, 764.

Page 10   SUBTRACTION

461, 381, 434, 374, 552, 512.

Page 11   QUICK QUESTIONS

1)10, 12, 15, 15, 14   2) 12, 18, 16, 14, 10
3) 19, 18, 17, 16, 20   4) 14, 18, 12, 13, 17
5) 9, 6, 7, 8, 4   6) 5, 6, 4, 7, 8
7) 20, 14, 14, 9, 10, 6, 20, 8, 12, 10, 13, 7, 14, 5, 17, 9, 8, 19, 9, 8.

Page 12   MULTIPLICATION TABLES

2, 4, 6, 8, 10, 12, 14, 16, 18, 20
3, 6, 9, 12, 15, 18, 21, 24, 27, 30
4, 8, 12, 16, 20, 24, 28, 32, 36, 40
5, 10, 15, 20, 25, 30, 35, 40, 45, 50
10, 20, 30, 40, 50, 60, 70, 80, 90, 100

Page 13   MORE MULTIPLICATION TABLES

(6,12,18), 24, 30, 36, 42, 48, 56, 60
(7), 14, 21, 28, 35, 42, 49, 56, 63, 70
(8), 16, 24, 32, 40, 48, 56, 64, 72, 80
(9), 18, 27, 36, 45, 54, 63, 72, 81, 90

Page 14   DIVIDING NUMBERS

9, 9, 4, 6, 4, 5, 8, 6, 9, 9, 4, 5
5 each, £8 each, 8 sweets each

Page 15   MEASURING CYLINDERS

310ml, 80ml, 400ml, 250ml, 490, 220ml.

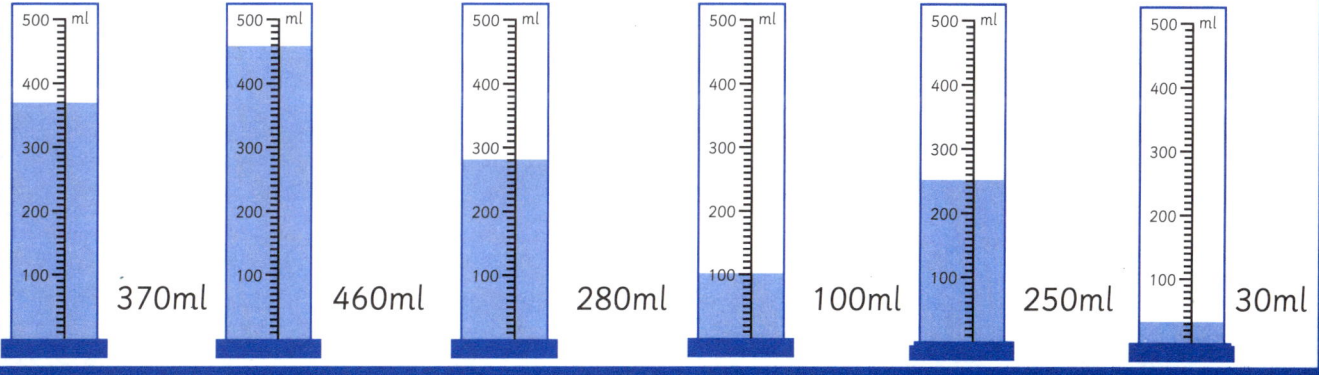

370ml   460ml   280ml   100ml   250ml   30ml

Page 17 TECHNICAL VOCABULARY

1. suffix 2. verb 3. rhyme 4. syllable 5. adverb 6. adjective 7. alliteration 8. tense 9. noun 10. prefix.

Page 18 SYLLABLES

billows(2), middle(2), sulkily(3), spoil(1), walrus(2), overhead(3), incredible(4), seven(2), conveniently(5), quantities(3), and(1), eager(2).
Poem verse 1,   (8), then 6, 8, 6, 8, 6.
Verse 2,   8, 6, 8, 6, 8, 6.

Page 19 RHYMING COUPLETS

tea, day, door, tree, here, dreaming.

Page 20 APOSTROPHES

1. The boy's book.
2. She wasn't very good at knitting.
3. My friend's pencil-case.
4. The car's engine.
5. My dad's trousers.
6. I won't go out today.
7. My sister's earrings.
8. He couldn't tie his shoelaces.

Page 21 ALPHABETICAL ORDER.

aeroplane, automobile, bicycle, bus, car, caravan, cart, coach, helicopter, lorry, motorbike, motorcycle, ship, submarine, taxi, trailer, train, tricycle, truck, yacht.
motorbike, motorcycle
helicopter, aeroplane, submarine, yacht, ship, train.

Page 22 COMMAS

1. Cows, pigs, goats, sheep, chickens, ducks and geese might all be found on a farm.
2. Dusting, polishing, washing and vacuuming all help to keep a home clean.
3. She went up the stairs, along the corridor and into the classroom.

Page 23 ADVERBS

walk   quickly, briskly, slowly

smile   cheerfully, happily, nervously

shout   angrily, loudly, crossly

verbs		adverbs	
	blazed		cheerfully
	swam		steadily
	shone		brightly
	barked, rang		loudly
	played		happily
	grows		quickly

Page 24 ALLITERATION

Examples: Alligators ate angry ants.
Cool cats climb curtains.
Dirty dogs dig ditches.
Enormous elephants entertain everyone.
Jumping jellyfish juggle jugs.
His hamster has hair.
Hot hippos hate hills.
My mouse mimics me.

Page 25 SUFFIXES

ment - agreement, appointment, entertainment, enjoyment.
ness - darkness, sadness, kindness, happiness
hood - childhood, brotherhood, neighbourhood, livelihood.
ship - hardship, partnership, championship, friendship.
ary - contrary, canary, library, dictionary
ic - fantastic, logic, music, magic.

Page 26 PREFIXES

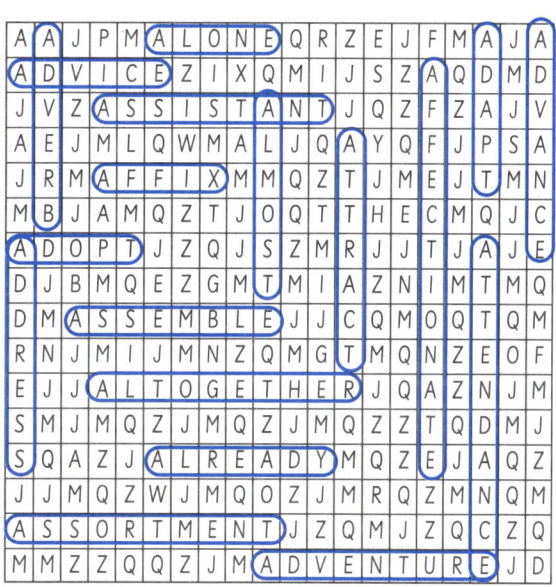

Sentence revealed: A PREFIX IS ALWAYS AT THE BEGINNING OF A WORD

Page 27 POWERFUL VERBS

walk   saunter, amble, stroll
fly   hover, soar, swoop
talk   whisper, mutter, shout
look   stare, glance, gaze

VERB TENSES

spoke, laughed, loved, bought, made
thought, ran, watched, washed, grinned.

Page 28 COMPREHENSION

1. three 2. watched, saw, darting 3. Tam, goldfish, pond, garden 4. e.g. quickly, happily, etc.
5. e.g. small, minute,
Dart - a sudden fast movement.

Page 30 THERMOMETERS

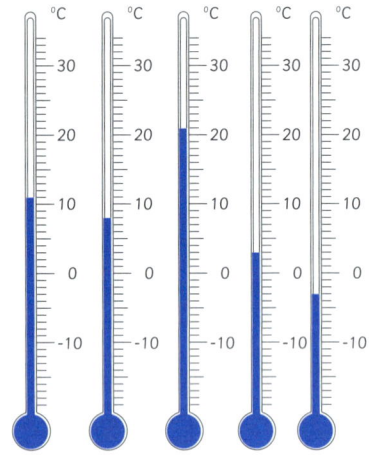

11°C, 8°C, 21°C, 3°C, -3°C.

Page 31 TEMPERATURE GRAPHS February 6°C, March 9°C, April 16°C, May 14°C, June 19°C, July 22°C, August 27°C, September 18°C, October 10°C, November 10°C, December 5°C. Hottest month - August, coldest - January.

Page 32 THE SKELETON 1. upper arm 2. backbone 3. pelvis 4. fingers 5. skull 6. ribs 7. forearm 8. kneecap 9. toes.

Page 33 Electric Circuits For the **bulb** to light up we need to make a complete **circuit**. We join one end of a wire to one side of the **bulb** holder using a **crocodile** clip. The other end of the **wire** is connected to one terminal of the **battery**. We use another wire to connect the other side of the bulb holder to the other terminal of the battery. 1. bulb, 2. bulb holder, 3. crocodile clip, 4. battery, 5. wire.

Page 34 ICT
Box 1. Jasdeep, Julie and Mary
Box 2. Wayne. Henry and Jim
Box 3. Jasdeep and Mary
Box 4. Julie Box 5. Henry   Box 6. Wayne and Jim

Page 36 THE ORCHESTRA Percussion - drum, xylophone, tambourine, glockenspiel, triangle, timpani, cymbals. Woodwind - bassoon, clarinet, flute, oboe. Brass - tuba, trombone, horn, trumpet. Strings - violin, double bass, cello, viola. Harp, violin, viola, cello, double bass. Flutes used to be made from wood.
Percussion, Woodwind, Brass and Strings.

Page 37 HISTORY Romans - Hadrian's Wall, chariot, Italy, Rome, centurion, legion. World War II - air raid, bombs, blitz, blackout, evacuee, rationing, gas mask. Vikings - Jorvik, longship, Norse, Scandinavia, Thor, Valhalla.
Valhalla, centurion, Scandinavia, gas mask, Italy, Rome.

Page 38 DIFFERENT RELIGIONS

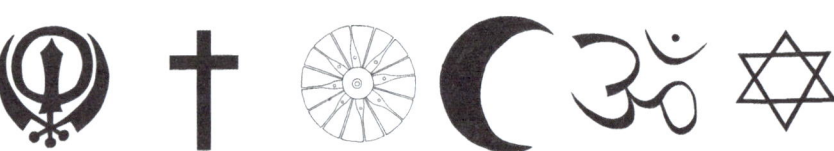

Sikhism, Christianity, Buddhism, Islam, Hinduism, Judaism

Page 39 THE COMPASS

East, South-West, North-East, South-East

Page 40 SCALE DRAWING
The Hall is 6cm long so it is really 12m long.
Mr Brown's classroom is 3cm long so it is really 6m long.
Mr Brown's classroom is 4cm wide so it is really 8m wide.

North
North-West
North-East
West
East
South-West
South-East
South

ALPHABETICAL ORDER

You may need a dictionary to help you to complete this page.
The words below are all connected with transport. Arrange them in alphabetical order.
You will need to take great care as some of the words have the same letters at the beginning.

tricycle	car	yacht	cart	lorry	bus
truck	taxi	caravan	trailer	ship	motorbike
aeroplane	bicycle	train	helicopter		
automobile	submarine	motorcycle	coach		

_____   _____   _____   _____

_____   _____   _____   _____

_____   _____   _____   _____

_____   _____   _____   _____

_____   _____   _____

Which two words mean the same?

_____   _____

Which six words describe vehicles that do not travel along roads?

_____   _____   _____

_____   _____   _____

COMMAS

Commas are needed when we write about lists of things. Look at this sentence about buying a list of fruits:

e.g. Please buy bananas, apples, plums and pears.

↑   ↑   ↑

We put commas here.   No comma because we are using the word **and** instead.

Rewrite the following sentences, putting commas in the correct places.

1   Cows pigs goats sheep chickens ducks and geese might all be found on a farm.

_____

_____

2   Dusting polishing washing and vacuuming all help to keep a home clean.

_____

_____

Try the next sentence. It needs one comma.

3   She went up the stairs along the corridor and into the classroom.

_____

_____

When you read the sentence out loud...

... you can hear where there should be a comma.

ADVERBS

An adverb is a word that describes a verb. Many adverbs end in ly.

Choose three adverbs from the box to describe each of the verbs below.

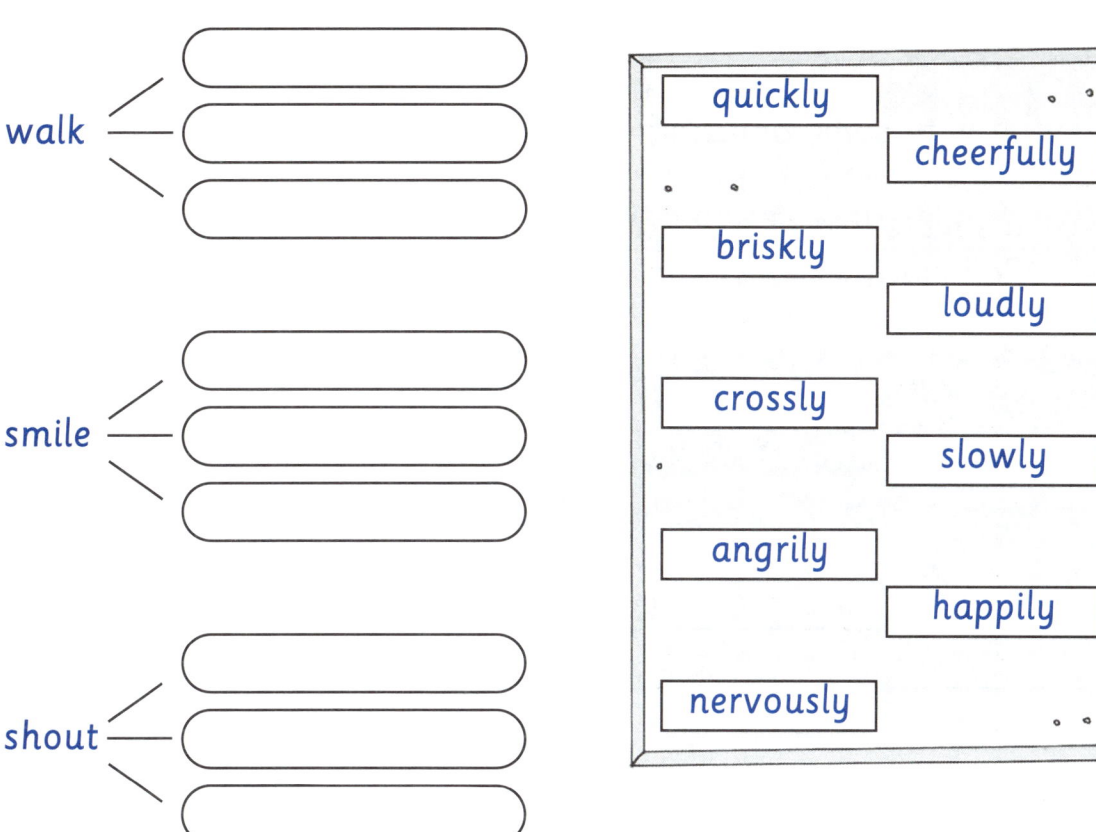

In each of the following sentences underline the verbs in blue and the adverbs in red.

The fire blazed cheerfully in the hearth.
The fish swam steadily along the river.
The star shone brightly in the dark sky.
The dog barked loudly when the doorbell rang.
She played happily in the garden.
Grass grows quickly in the summer.

ALLITERATION

Alliteration uses words that begin with the same sound.
It is often found in poetry and tongue-twisters.

> Here is an example: Dizzy ducks sometimes dance delightfully.
> Notice that most of the words begin with the letter d.

Have fun with some amazing animal alliteration.

Invent a simple line of alliteration for each of the following creatures.
Use a dictionary to check the spelling of all new words you use.

cat	dog	hippo	hamster
	elephant		alligator
duck		jellyfish	mouse

SUFFIXES

A suffix is a word ending.
Sort the words from the box below according to their suffixes.

agreement   logic   darkness   hardship

sadness   partnership   appointment

canary   championship   entertainment   contrary

library   kindness   music   childhood

brotherhood   dictionary   friendship   enjoyment

magic   happiness   fantastic

neighbourhood   livelihood

ment

ness

hood

ship

ary

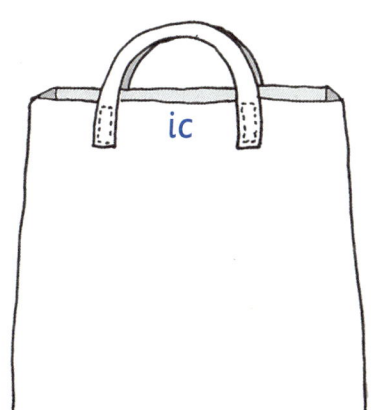

ic

PREFIXES

A word beginning is called a **prefix**.

The words in the box below start with the prefixes **ad**, **al**, **ass**, **aff** and **att**.

adverb	adopt	altogether	affix	adapt
almost	address	attract	assistant	
adventure	already	attendance	alone	advice
advance	assemble	assortment	affectionate	

The words from the box are all in the word search below.
Find the words and lightly shade them.

A	A	J	P	M	A	L	O	N	E	Q	R	Z	E	J	F	M	A	J	A
A	D	V	I	C	E	Z	I	X	Q	M	I	J	S	Z	A	Q	D	M	D
J	V	Z	A	S	S	I	S	T	A	N	T	J	Q	Z	F	Z	A	J	V
A	E	J	M	L	Q	W	M	A	L	J	Q	A	Y	Q	F	J	P	S	A
J	R	M	A	F	F	I	X	M	M	Q	Z	T	J	M	E	J	T	M	N
M	B	J	A	M	Q	Z	T	J	O	Q	T	T	H	E	C	M	Q	J	C
A	D	O	P	T	J	Z	Q	J	S	Z	M	R	J	J	T	J	A	J	E
D	J	B	M	Q	E	Z	G	M	T	M	I	A	Z	N	I	M	T	M	Q
D	M	A	S	S	E	M	B	L	E	J	J	C	Q	M	O	Q	T	Q	M
R	N	J	M	I	J	M	N	Z	Q	M	G	T	M	Q	N	Z	E	O	F
E	J	J	A	L	T	O	G	E	T	H	E	R	J	Q	A	Z	N	J	M
S	M	J	M	Q	Z	J	M	Q	Z	J	M	Q	Z	Z	T	Q	D	M	J
S	Q	A	Z	J	A	L	R	E	A	D	Y	M	Q	Z	E	J	A	Q	Z
J	J	M	Q	Z	W	J	M	Q	O	Z	J	M	R	Q	Z	M	N	Q	M
A	S	S	O	R	T	M	E	N	T	J	Z	Q	M	J	Z	Q	C	Z	Q
M	M	Z	Z	Q	Q	Z	J	M	A	D	V	E	N	T	U	R	E	J	D

Now colour all the extra letters j, m, q, y and z.
If you have done this correctly the remaining letters should spell out a useful message.
Write the message here.

_ _____

_ _   _____   _ _   ___

_____   _ _   _   ___

POWERFUL VERBS

Using powerful verbs can make your writing more interesting.
Here are some interesting verbs.

saunter	shout	gaze	amble
hover	soar	stroll	stare
whisper	mutter	glance	swoop

From the words in the box choose three powerful verbs that could be used instead of each of the more ordinary verbs below.

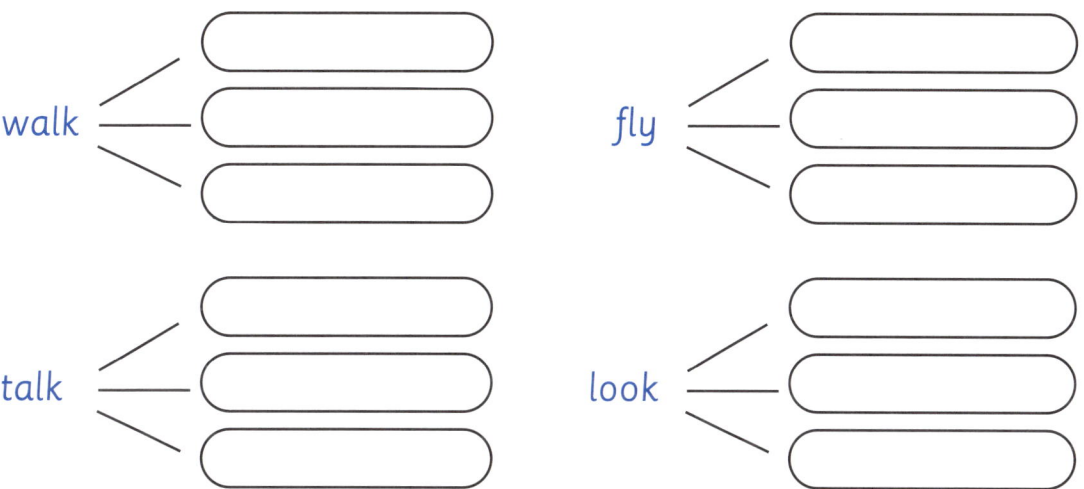

walk

fly

talk

look

VERB TENSES

Each of the following verbs is in the present tense.
Write its past tense beside it. The first two have been done for you.
Many, but not all, verbs have ed added when they are written in the past tense.
Use a dictionary to help you to write each of the past tenses correctly.

say	said	talk	talked
speak		think	
laugh		run	
love		watch	
buy		wash	
make		grin	

COMPREHENSION

Read this text **carefully**.

Tam watched the three small goldfish in the little pond in the garden. He saw them darting in and out of the weeds, their scales flashing in the sunlight. When he scattered food on the water the fish immediately came towards the surface. Each time one of them snatched a piece of food there was a tiny splash. Again and again this happened until the food was finished. Tam loved to watch the fish and felt he would never tire of it.

Now answer the questions below. You may need a dictionary or a thesaurus to help you.

1 How many goldfish were in the pond? ☐

2 Write the first three verbs in the text.

☐ ☐ ☐

3 Write the four nouns that are in the first sentence.

☐ ☐ ☐ ☐

4 Name an adverb that could follow the word darting to make the second sentence more interesting.

☐

5 Name two other adjectives that you think could have been used instead of the word **tiny** in sentence four.

☐ ☐

6 Use a dictionary to help you to write a definition for the following word as used in the text.

Dart

_____

_____

_____

_____

The National curriculum shows that every child in Year 4 needs to be taught Science and the 'foundation subjects', Art, Design Technology, Geography, History, Information Technology, Music and Physical Education, together with Religious Education.

✔ SCIENCE

During Year 4, your child will experience work on:
- collecting evidence to test their prediction;
- designing fair scientific tests;
- making observations and taking measurements of temperature, length, time and force;
- presenting results using tables or bar charts;
- identifying trends in results shown on tables, charts or graphs.

The scientific topics will include:
- Moving and Growing, particularly in relation to bones and skeletons;
- Habitats;
- Keeping Warm;
- Solids, liquids and how they can be separated;
- Friction;
- Circuits and Conductors.

✔ DESIGN TECHNOLOGY

In Year 4, children will continue to develop their skills in designing and constructing using a variety of materials.

They will examine purses, wallets and other containers for money, then make their own. They will design and make a paper item using moving parts. This is most likely to be a pop-up book with moving parts operated by linkage and levers. Alternative items are greetings cards, puppets or posters with moving parts. They will learn about electrical circuits to design and make a simple alarm system or a simple lighting system. They will experiment with different switches, connecting them to batteries by using wires and clips.

✔ INFORMATION TECHNOLOGY

The children will:
- use word processing skills to produce pieces of writing, experimenting with different font sizes and styles of font, moving sections of text using cut and paste techniques and checking work by using the spell-check;
- use a graphics package to produce images that incorporate repeated patterns, possibly making use of a digital camera, a scanner or clip art;
- sort information using branching databases;
- create and interpret bar charts, pie charts and line graphs using data handling software;
- operate a simple robot such as a floor turtle; work on the computer using a 'screen turtle' to draw specific shapes.

Get Ready for Year 4 Science, IT and DT Information for Adults

THERMOMETERS

This thermometer shows a temperature of twenty-five degrees Celsius.

This would be a nice warm day in summer.

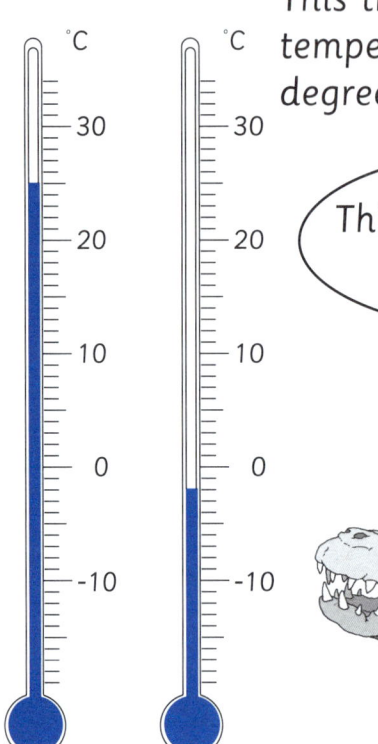

This thermometer shows a temperature of minus two degrees Celsius

This would be a cold day in winter.

Show the temperatures on these thermometers:

| 11°C | 8°C | 21°C | 3°C | -3°C |

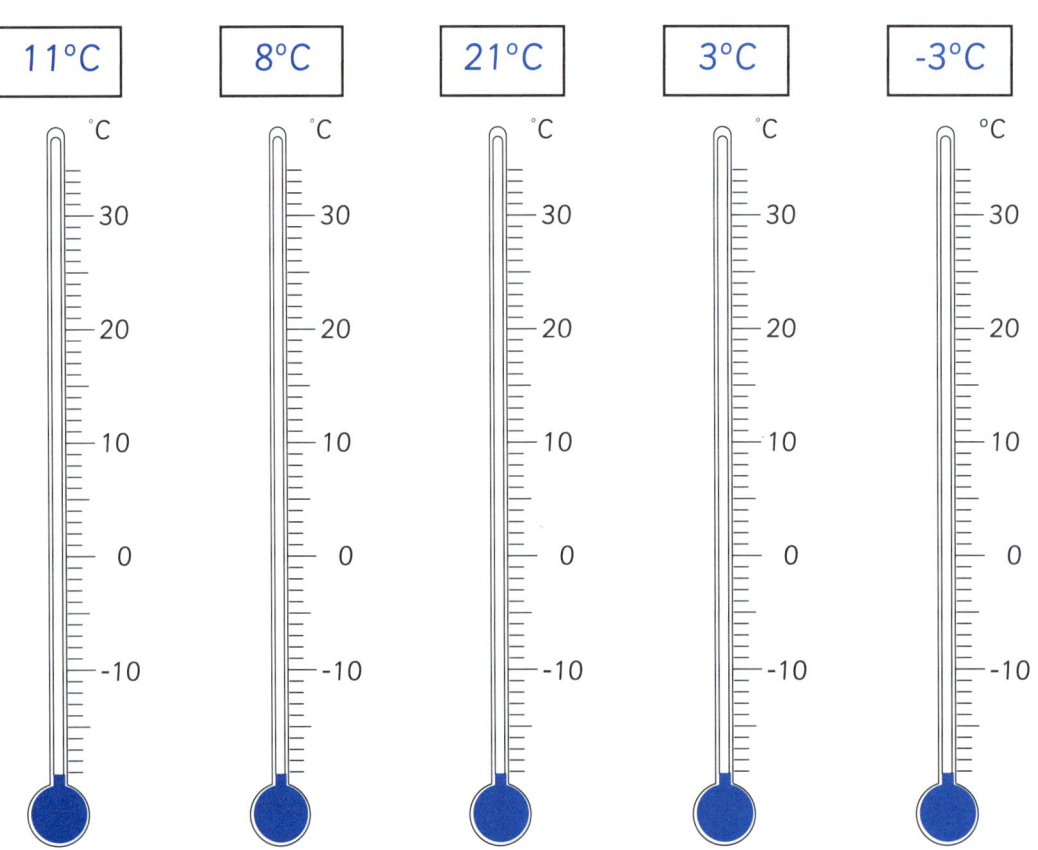

Watch the weather forecast on television.
What is the temperature forecast for tomorrow?

TEMPERATURE GRAPHS

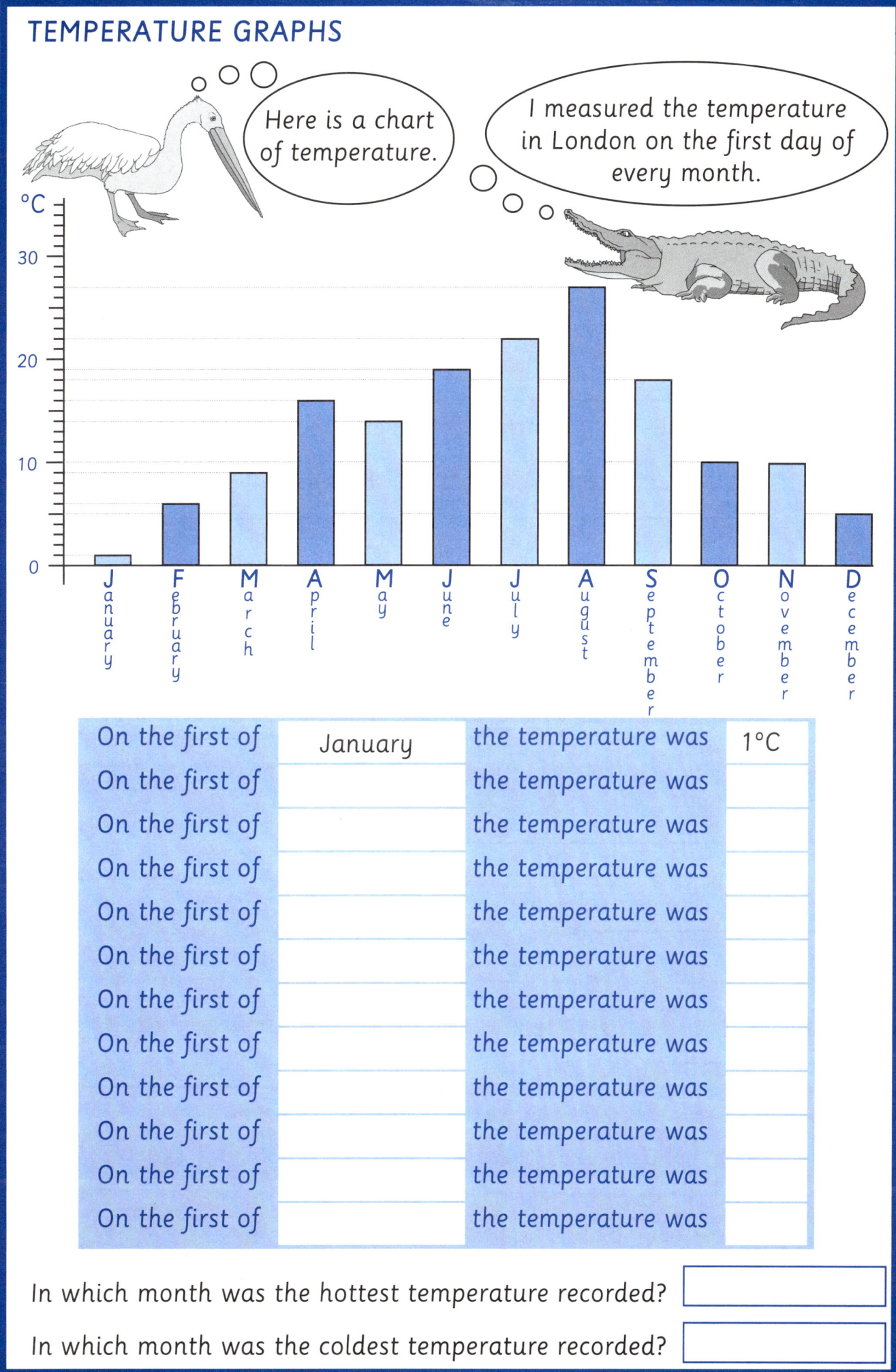

Here is a chart of temperature.

I measured the temperature in London on the first day of every month.

On the first of	January	the temperature was	1°C
On the first of		the temperature was	
On the first of		the temperature was	
On the first of		the temperature was	
On the first of		the temperature was	
On the first of		the temperature was	
On the first of		the temperature was	
On the first of		the temperature was	
On the first of		the temperature was	
On the first of		the temperature was	
On the first of		the temperature was	
On the first of		the temperature was	

In which month was the hottest temperature recorded? ☐

In which month was the coldest temperature recorded? ☐

THE SKELETON

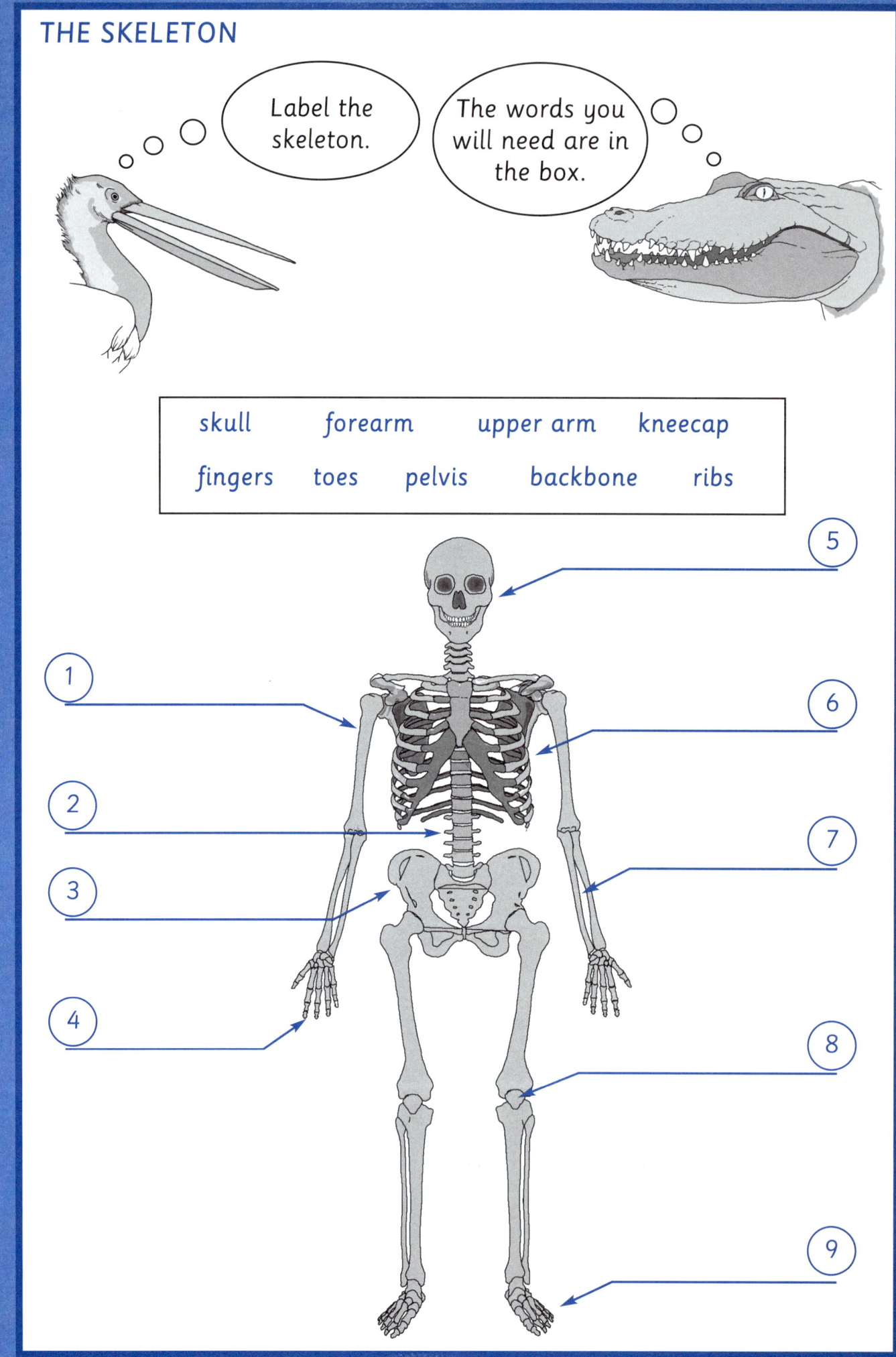

Label the skeleton.

The words you will need are in the box.

skull	forearm	upper arm	kneecap
fingers	toes	pelvis	backbone	ribs

ELECTRIC CIRCUITS

Here are the words you will need on this page:

bulb	wire	circuit	wires	crocodile clip
crocodile	clips	battery		bulb holder

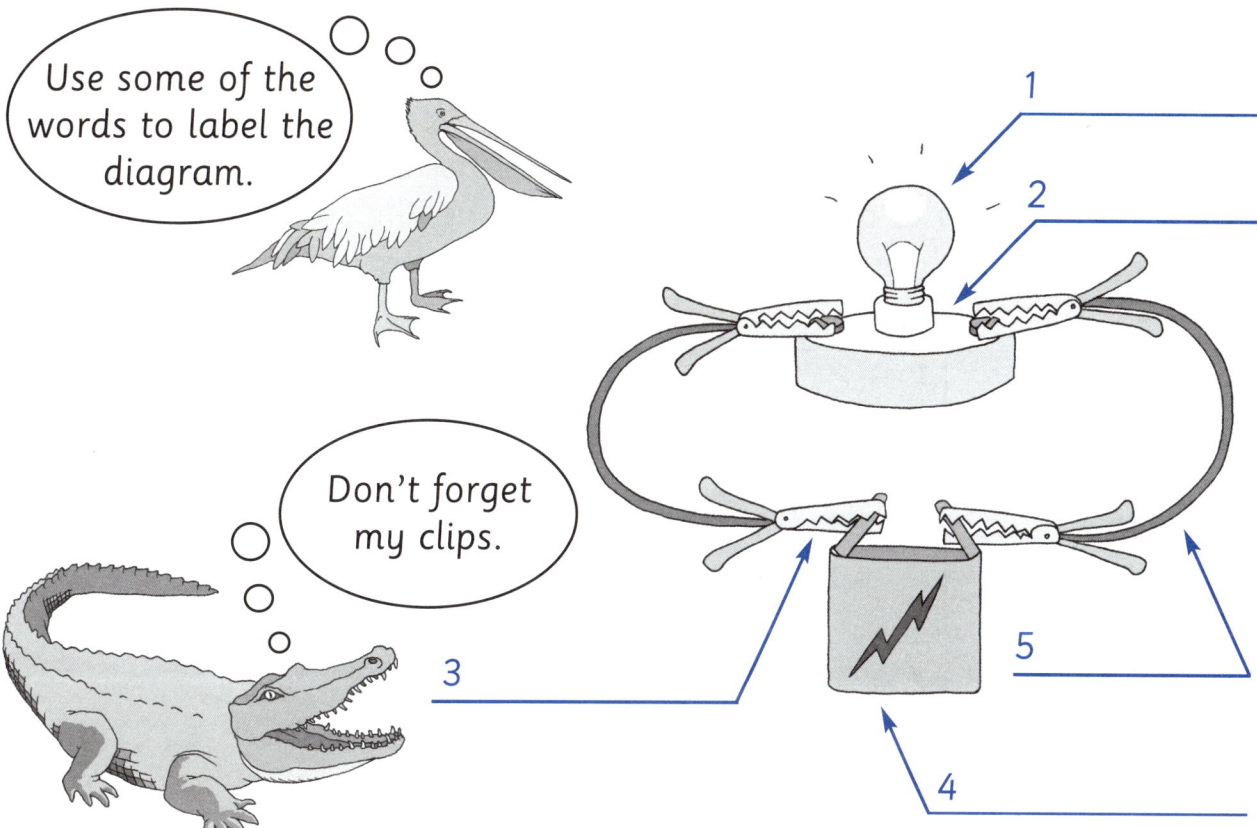

Use some of the words to label the diagram.

Don't forget my clips.

1

2

3

4

5

Now use some of the words to fill the gaps:

For the _____ to light up we need to make a complete

_____ . We join one end of a wire to one side of the

_____ holder using a _____ clip. The other

end of the _____ is connected to one terminal of the

battery. We use another wire to connect the other side of the bulb

holder to the other terminal of the _____ .

INFORMATION AND COMMUNICATION TECHNOLOGY

Jasdeep
Age 9

Wayne
Age 36

Julie
Age 42

Henry
Age 8

Mary
Age 6 months

Jim
Age 57

We can sort the people in the pictures using a branching chart with questions to answer. List the names in the correct boxes.

Is the person female?

YES

NO

1

2

Is the person a child?

YES

NO

YES

NO

3

4

5

6

There should be two names in here: the female children.

There should be one name in here: the female adult.

There should be one name in here: the male child.

There should be two names in here: the male adults.

✔ **MUSIC**

During Year 4 children will continue to develop and extend their musical understanding in a variety of ways. The work in this book introduces knowledge of the instruments of the orchestra.

✔ **R.E.**

During Year 4 children will develop their understanding of the major world religions. This is aided in this book by work on the symbol that represents each of six major faiths.

✔ **HISTORY**

In Year 4 pupils will be building on the historical skills developed in Years 1 to 3. They may focus on Invaders and Settlers, The Tudors and the life of a child during World War II.

✔ **ART**

In Years 3 and 4, children will experience work on:
- Portraits which show relationships.
- Patterns in textiles and printing, from different cultures and times.
- Sculpture, examining sculpture in public places and making their own.
- Viewpoints in the school to create artwork on the subject of a dream.
- Designing and making model chairs.
- Drawing, painting, printing and collage to produce artwork about a journey.

✔ **GEOGRAPHY**

During their geography work in Year 4 pupils will:
- Learn about the eight points of the compass.
- Begin to use scales on maps.
- Use atlases, plans, maps and globes.
- Consider how to improve the area they can see from the window. They may use the school, its grounds and the nearby locality to consider environmental issues. They will also look at the settlements in the school's area when considering how they spend their leisure and recreation time.
- Link to work in history, studying settlements in villages.
- Study a village in India (though some schools may choose to study another overseas location).

✔ **PHYSICAL EDUCATION**

Your child will experience work in dance, athletics, gymnastics and 'invasion games'. Invasion games include games such as football or netball where the players have to enter the other players' area to score goals. The children will not always take part in full games but will practise the necessary skills in pairs or small groups.

In some schools the Year 4 pupils will also learn skills for 'striking' games such as cricket or rounders. They may also have swimming lessons.

THE ORCHESTRA
FASCINATING FACTS TO READ.

1 A large modern orchestra may have more than 100 musicians.

2 The earliest flutes were made of wood.

3 The harp has 47 strings and 7 foot pedals.

Read up and down this grid to find 19 instruments that are used in an orchestra. Write the name of each instrument in the correct section below.

start here

D	O	L	E	C	B	L	E	G	I	A	P	A
R	I	I	N	L	U	E	T	L	R	N	M	N
U	V	N	I	A	O	B	U	O	T	G	I	I
M	E	B	R	R	D	A	L	C	A	L	T	C
T	N	A	U	I	E	S	F	K	L	E	T	Y
U	O	S	O	N	N	S	N	E	O	O	E	M
B	H	S	B	E	O	C	R	N	I	B	P	B
A	P	O	M	T	B	E	O	S	V	O	M	A
X	O	O	A	T	M	L	H	P	L	E	U	L
Y	L	N	T	R	O	L	O	I	E	T	R	S

Percussion	Woodwind	Brass	Strings
	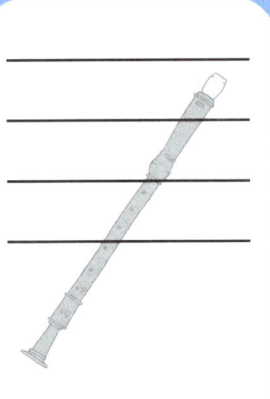	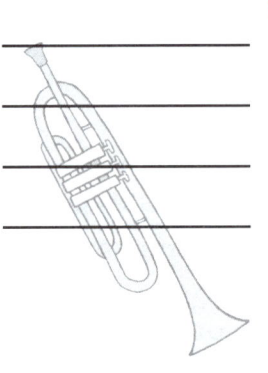	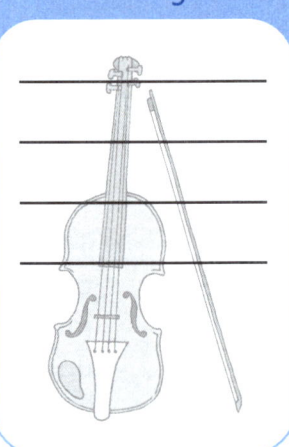

Use what you have learned on this page to answer the questions below:

♪ Name 5 stringed instruments.

_____ _____ _____ _____ _____

♪ Why is the flute in the woodwind section of the orchestra when it is made of metal?

_____

♪ Name the 4 sections of the orchestra.

_____ _____ _____ _____

HISTORY

Put the words from the box into the correct 'books'.

Jorvik   air raid   bombs
    Hadrian's Wall   chariot   Norse
Italy   blitz   blackout
    Valhalla   evacuee   rationing   longship
legion   Thor   Rome
    gas mask   centurion   Scandinavia

ROMANS   WORLD WAR II   VIKINGS

Choose a word from above to fill each of the spaces in the sentences below.

The Viking heaven was called ————————————————.

A ———————————— was a Roman officer who commanded 100 men.

The Vikings came from ———————————————— in their longships.

In World War II everyone was required to carry a ————————————.

The Romans came from ———————————— , a country with a capital

city called————————————.

DIFFERENT RELIGIONS

In your neighbourhood there could be different people who belong to a number of different religions.

Would you recognise the symbol of each main religion?

Carefully read the clues to help you label each symbol correctly.

Religion	Clue
Buddhism →	An eight-spoked wheel.
Christianity →	A cross.
Judaism →	A six-pointed star.
Islam →	A crescent.
Hinduism →	Eastern written symbol.
Sikhism →	A double-edged sword inside a circle, on the outside of which are two curved swords.

  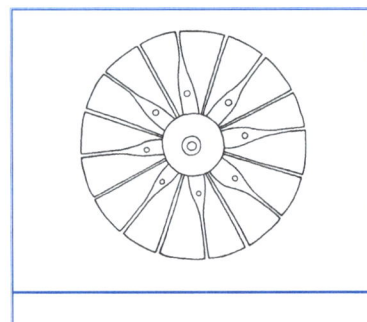

  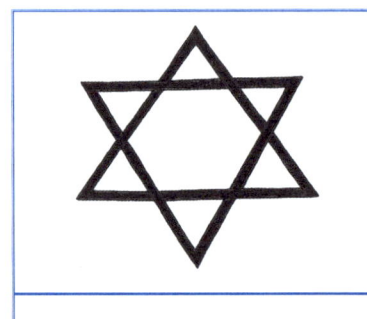

THE COMPASS

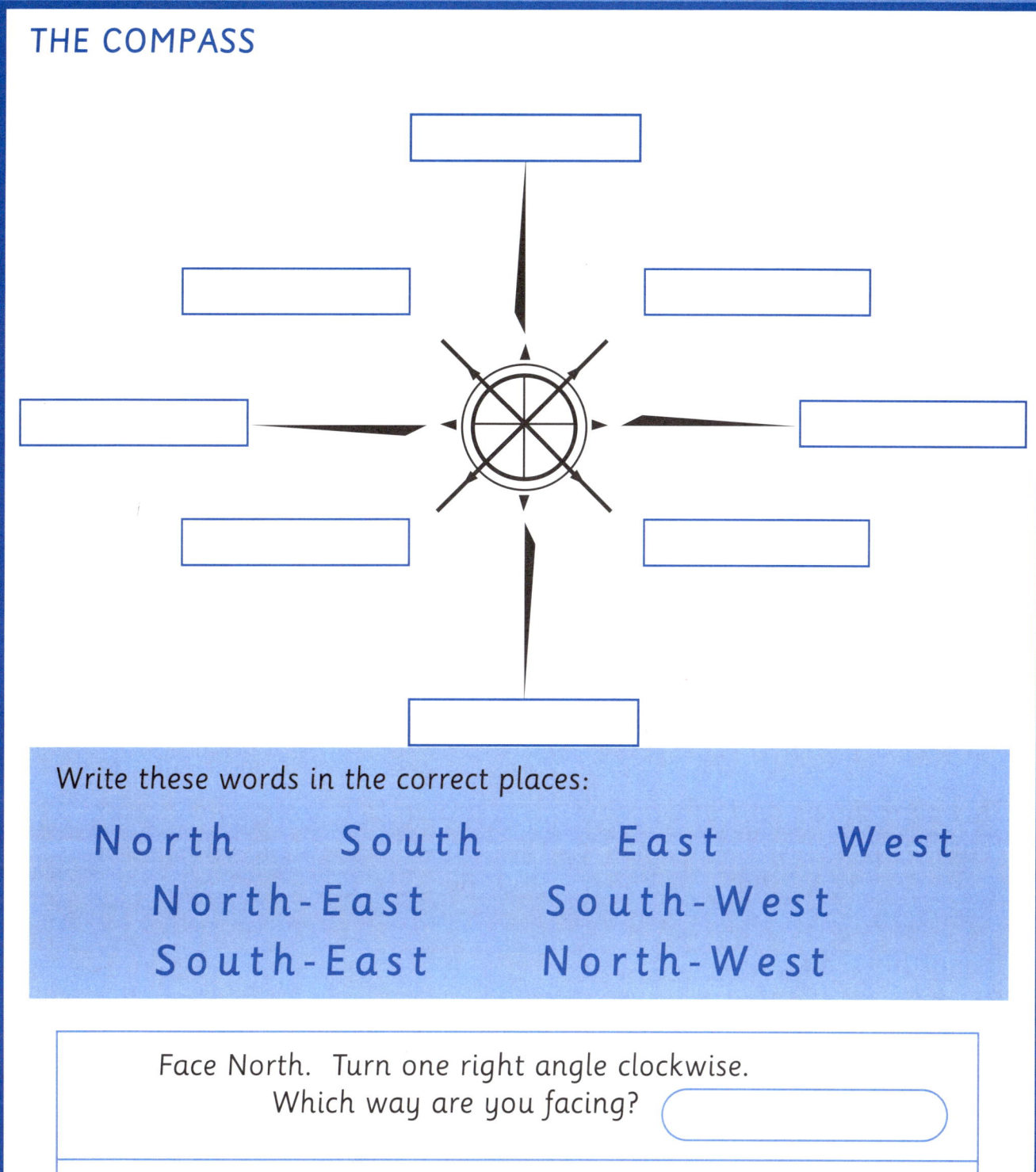

Write these words in the correct places:

North   South   East   West
North-East   South-West
South-East   North-West

Face North. Turn one right angle clockwise.
Which way are you facing?

Face South-East. Turn one right angle clockwise.
Which way are you facing?

Face South-East. Turn one right angle anti-clockwise.
Which way are you facing?

Face North-West. Turn two right angles clockwise.
Which way are you facing?

SCALE DRAWING

Plan of St. John's School

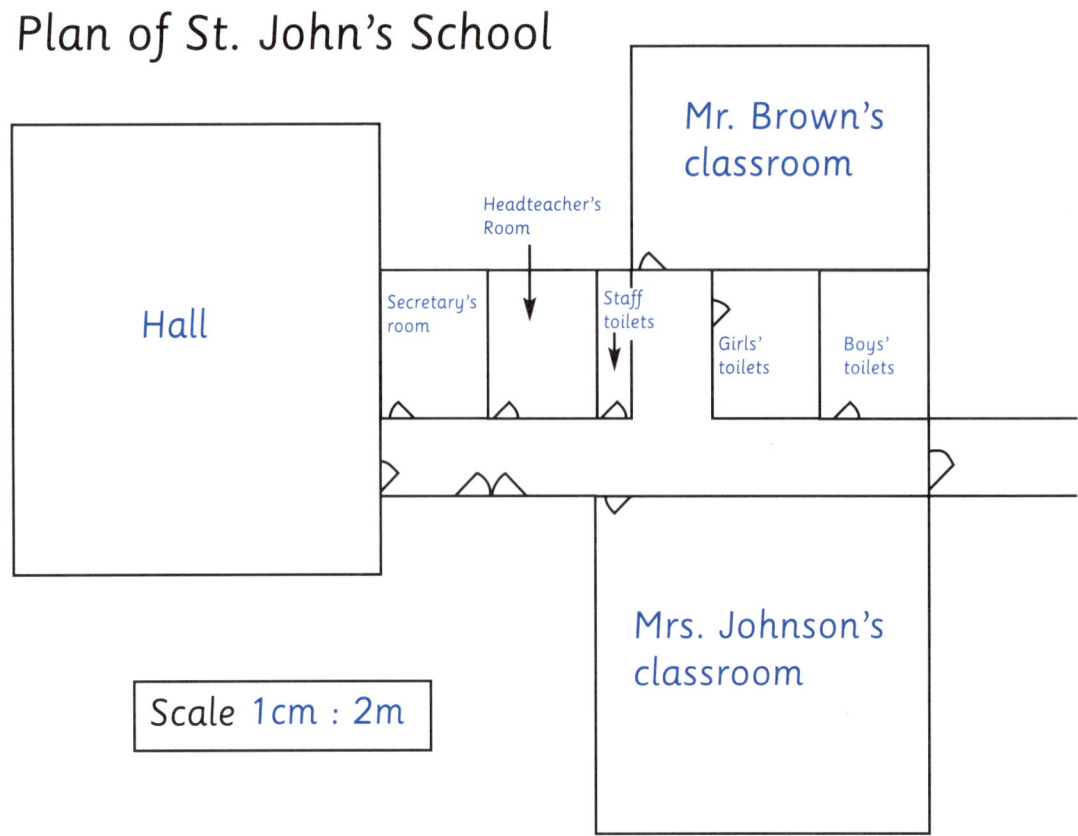

Scale 1cm : 2m

This plan shows part of a school. It is drawn to a scale where one centimetre represents two metres. We show this scale like this:

    1cm : 2m   (<u>or</u> 1 : 200 because 2m = 200cm)

Using this scale:

On the plan, the Hall measures 5 centimetres wide. This means that it is really 10 metres wide because every centimetre on the plan is really worth two metres.

Try these:

On the plan,

    … the Hall is ☐ cm long so it is really ☐ m long.

    … Mr Brown's classroom is ☐ long so it is really ☐ long.

    … Mr Brown's classroom is ☐ wide so it is really ☐ wide.

Try measuring some of the other rooms. Find their sizes in centimetres on the plan, then work out their real sizes. Remember that 1cm on the plan is worth 2m in the real school.